Why I Live in the Forest

The Wesleyan Poetry Program: Volume 74

Why I Live in the Forest

by

James Nolan

WESLEYAN UNIVERSITY PRESS

Middletown, Connecticut

MIDDLEBURY COLLEGE LIBRARY

I want to thank Louis Simpson especially for his generous and thought-
ful editorial guidance and to acknowledge with gratitude the support
of the Ossabaw Island Project and of the State of California.

— James Nolan

Copyright © 1974 by James Nolan

Acknowledgement is gratefully made to Word Books for permission
to reprint in this book the two poems entitled 'The Cross and the
Weathercock' and 'Tyger! Tyger!', which were originally published in
1971 in *Adam Among the Television Trees*, an anthology edited by
Virginia R. Mollenkott.

Library of Congress Cataloging in Publication Data

Nolan, James, 1947–
    Why I live in the forest.

    (The Wesleyan poetry program: v. 74)
    Poems.
    I. Title.
    PS3564.036W5   811'.5'4   74–5967
    ISBN 0-8195-2074-8
    ISBN 0-8195-1074-2 (pbk.)

PS
3564
036
W5

Manufactured in the United States of America
First edition

for Harriette and Kinga

Contents

Why I Live in the Forest

Leaving Homes

for my sister

O. K. You've broken through again
pecking through the dollhouse's sky
that kept you safe   wifely and demure
as you made it through the porcelain
of Mother's shut-in teacup world
shattering that hometown family
bit to sharp and brittle shards
that cut you still   visiting the folks
treading with a wince on broken eggshells.

So your husband the Bayou Squire
was sent packing   leaving his baby-doll
paternally a freezerful of squirrel meat
he trapped himself (the pretty things)
like he trapped you.

                Now you study
scented books on Zen and Krishna;
you study love (and I can't recommend
a book on that) as you relish its release.
You file divorce papers. You wear all black
a bright serape draped around your turtleneck
as if to say my joy is wrapped around me
like an evening daiquiri   a party dip.
It does not live inside.

Chainsmoking   you talk of your psychiatrist
using the sturdy beams of jargon he builds
your new house with. Excavating old ruins

and raising false Sistine ceilings   Sister
an Oedipal touch to bottle all this airy stuff —
"What else *can* I be? A teepee in the wind?"
Always this doom of domed rooms rising up
all around you but some wild glint
in the eye catches a speck of sky and
you must follow it down dark corridors
shaky   half-believing   but wanting out:
until your find yourself in glaring light
under the Big Tent in the Big Time at last
stepping out onto the tightrope of your freedom
as the crowd gasps and mothers and fathers
husbands and bald shrinks grow faint. . . .

Patricia   breaking through is lifetime's work.
Most crouch like cliffdwellers in cubicles
some crash like Icarus — the dashy ones:
few really ever know the color of the sky.
What a slow slow soar out of yourself
it is into that grace above the clouds
where all is possible: your dance   your love.

I shiver to see you in that cavern I know so well
the solitude that soothes the shock of flight
to see you slouched in bed
walled-in by books on *who* & *how* & *why*.
But I am full of hope
and also sometimes fear
whenever I see the slumped shoulders

of your canary-colored shawl
start   rise   and push impetuously out
the just-sprung door of your cage
to make a do-or-die bee-line dive
toward the wide blue sky
on the other side
of the glass window pane.

Don't hurt yourself this way.

Return to the House of Scorpio

Walking again down Canal Street
in this seething Scorpio city:
you never really leave New Orleans
you only dream you do.

With surprise attacks
of comfort I sit back —
can manoeuver drunk
the inkwell spiral stairs

a struck match throwing Fellini
shadows against the peeling walls.
Under high superstitious ceilings
I reach right for the *café au lait*

there where hot red peppers dry
strung along the kitchen mantel.
I even know the black cat by name:
come here . . . minou . . . minou.

The smell of garlic and onions
of oysters and steaming red beans!
And where have I heard that
tough Brooklyn talk before?

New Orleans: I can see you
fading ageing whore you are
Blanche DuBois in a pinafore
primping in the armoire mirror —

crow's-feet in amber lantern light.
Mother   through every half-shut
shutter I see your marquisette face
in damp courtyards of hydrangea

and Father   it's your voice I hear
call down around Magazine Street
when my cheeks are flushing red
in some boozy Irish brawl.

15

Flopped Mayonnaise

Chère Karen: *Infatué* with your French ways
today I tried to make mayonnaise using
peanut oil. The yolks sank to the bottom.

You see I'm from the South. The next time
we're in Paris we must sit by the Seine
whistle Dixie and eat a sweet potato.

Anima Drag

If I were a woman
I would want to be
a cold beauty like Garbo
and throw rambunctious
orgies in fringed cabanas
by the sea with Turks   Greeks
and tall Negresses in blue

turbans with many bracelets
and when the police vans
arrived at five of dawn
stare them away
with the Evil Eye
like an agate through
my wrought-iron fence.

If I were a woman
I would not lash myself
to some sea-sick family
but would give love
without apology:
charge in your door
at 4:00 in the morning

in green leotards to read
Blake out loud while you
defrosted the refrigerator.
If I were a woman
I would hate men
and would probably be
a lesbian   sleeping

only with young boys
and older   more mature women.
If I were a woman
I would sit spaced in all-night
places in a wide straw hat
waiting to meet a man like me
the kind of man that I could be

if I were loved by a woman like me.

Lady of the Rope

Et ta bouche couleur de meurtre,
Et tes sens couleur de désert,
O Salomé de mes Hontes,
Salomé!
—*Milosz*, Poèmes de la Décadence

Lady of the Rope pays me a visit
caked scarlet under long fingernails
hair peaked and rampant in the air.
There's smoke on her breath   heavy
cigarette smoke rasps from her throat
musking the hyacinth smell of her neck
where she wears her corsage of nooses.

Lady of the Rope is suddenly there
perfect as only a vampiress can be
whose lips touch lips that touch food
but lets her lovers do the digesting
the eating and breathing and burning as
she plays with her vials of strong essence.
She slips behind ears her coquettish lasso

of fingers. Turned-on in a trance I follow.
Lady of the Rope is still but in flight.
Her face is a faceless Winged Victory
She shows me a place I can pose as a statue
a shrine in a grotto with a tiny glass door
and she holds the key. She tells me they'll pass
with bowed heads thinking such thoughts of me

and I a post in the waves of procession
shall not waver but stand as a god.
Lady of the Rope is undressing me
her cool hands tingle my feverish skin
and I slide into arms as into a shirt.
But her breath is the sandstorm of ages
her cunt is a powdery well   her breasts

baggies of ashes. I'm hanging in spasms
but coming in all the wrong ways. A dry-
dream: I'm awake. Her rope cut   she leaves
tripping a ripple of breeze through the trees.
Her rope is this necktie I try on each morning
glance in the mirror   and then put away.

Morning Meditation #33

Waking at 4
in the after-
(it all) noon of
another nude day

half-dressed
by the shadows
of window shades
I sit up in bed

and watch the sun
hestitate on rooftops
held at the horizon
by a dandy's kid glove.

Clothes and papers
misplaced everywhere:
whatever it is
I'm doing

my heart's not in it.

How

We meet 1 little 2
little 3 little Indians
in the redwood forest
who have just stepped off
42nd Street with bottles

of cheap wine wrapped
in brown paper bags.
They stand smirking
pitching rocks at
the blacktop road

while we speed off
on our silver mustang.
Gas-station cowboys
a prime-time posse
of the dispossessed

in their pointy black
boots and tight levi's
with sniggers of hate
and fear: they are
where we were and we

whipping across the hills
our long hair under beaded headbands
our long hair leaping in Apache air.

Poem about Straw

for Ginny

I shut you in my bed that night
like the princess in the castle
to spin my room of straw to gold
with your wide hips   love's handles.
Spinning-jenny   cotton ginny
we spun all night to turn
the straw to bolts of gold
that streamed in through the window

at dawn when the princess changed
her last straw to coin for the king
and the Jews rose to mix the batch
of straw to brick for Pharaoh's tomb
in the desert where the camel's back
was broken by that last straw and he
leapt through the eye of a needle
moving mustard seeds and mountains
of straw
hats and alligator shoes
the princess wore

on the beach   after breakfast
when we walked hand to handle
straw wound with gold in our hair.

The Cross and the Weathercock

St. Peter's   the old angelic church
so good and all so central
needs the cross and weathercock
put back upon its steeple
(where all such symbols of import
respectfully return if able.)
The poor Turks   the poor Irish
the pale abandoned child
(no doubt a case of bastardy)
scarcely have the wheat to eat
much less the Will to Be
for the heavy hand of God
has laid its big fat finger
on the land this year

but the weathercock spins wide-chested in the wind
and the cross folds its two iron arms
in silent resignation.

Stephanie's Story

After it all
after I give up sex
am given up by my children

after I lose the men
am lost from the wanting
perhaps while I go grey

under the striped awning
of a cottage in New Mexico
living alone in the desert

like Georgia O'Keefe
beneath a clear unframed sky
a light open space on top

all the clutter on the shelf

I shall write my autobiography
No More Convulsions.

The Streetlight and the Moon

The moon rises with a stocking
stretched over its face taunting
now you see me now you don't.

The streetlight flicks on at 6
and off at 6 bearing down with
the same steady flood-lit stare.

The moon and the streetlight
the streetlight and the moon:
every night this variety routine

the fall-guy making faces while
the straight-man just stands there.
Every night this bright duet

and you ask me what to do?
Don't show your dreams
to the streetlight

love
don't drive your car
to the moon.

Modern Times

I have never signed
the peace pact with machinery
never can open car doors
or even a can for that matter.

I peck my way through typewriters
smudging and swearing like a coalminer
and always wind up with tape-recorders
like an Englishman eating spaghetti.

The Indians signed it
and see what happened to them
herded by tractors onto reservations;
the immigrants signed it

and were stuffed into canneries
to baby-sit conveyor belts.
The President has signed it
even the Pope has signed it

but I will never sign
the peace pact with machinery
I will fight it tooth and throttle.
Every car that turns up my drive

is always carried off on a stretcher.
My record-players become deaf mutes
my glare makes TVs catatonic and
vacuum cleaners bite the dust.

I live in a quiet rain forest
with no car and much license
where even the egg-beater
is not my best friend.

Night Vegetables

The fat yellow pan moon
looks good as an omelette.
Rising it cries *eat me*   *eat me*
while the stones on the shore
bask and glimmer thick and smooth
like a sea of boiled potatoes.

All night I sit up in the kitchen
near the stove with a black mushroom
hat and my steel-grey fish-eye cat
mixing a batch of salamander soup
in a teapot: I am the night cook.
I stir and bake while you sleep.

Every night I am busy till dawn
rattling pots and pans in your pillow.
I am the short-order cook of your dreams
filling silver bowls with scorpions
heads   snakes   lovely women and trees
a dredged-up deep-sea jambalaya
which I serve at the head of your bed
in bowls which flatten out as you wake
into those round white porcelain plates
of eggs and cereal which you gobble fast.

By day I am invisible   a thin smile
in the corner of the four walls
you have worked all your life to live in:
the hot and concrete hunger of the sun
where you have learned to get by
to walk quickly and to ask less
while the steady glow at the center

of your reading-lamp brain is burned out
by the bare light bulb that beats down
day by day   which you lean over to flick off
as I step in with my white hair
and silver skin and trembling tray.

There is someone who comes
in the night all children know
and are so wishful or afraid:
sandman   Santa Claus   boogeyman
good fairy   leprechaun   dream man.
He stands in the kitchen stirring
the dark with a long silver spoon.

I feed the other side of your eyes
facing the faces inside of your head.
And *you*   no you do not know me
do not see me   nor do you know why
on waking to the hunger of the sun
you sit up   and feel well fed.

The White Townhouse

I cannot live in your white townhouse
with its polished brass lamps and long green lawn.
I cannot live in this aquarium room
this glass birdcage   this tree-house room
where you come to be you   to play free.

I cannot be your mythical pet
with gremlin cheeks and unicorn hair
a leprechaun man   a holy-grail man   a comet
pulling legs and having visions and making altars.
I am so very sick of being Shiva
my thousand arms waving
in a thousand different places
tangling together like thick artery-red
lines on a map   clotting together everywhere
at once and nowhere really at all.

It has been good being here for a while
after the woozy tunnel of travel I've done
like falling weightless from corner to corner
in a room without gravity   a wild carnival ride

but I cannot live in your white townhouse
with you and your healthy lawyer-lover
who makes me smoke his pipe and talk turkey
who tamps his pipe and chuckles at the cat.

No I did not expect you to stay where you were
that dirty sock   that one-room cage in Manhattan
police-locked and four flights up   stale smoke
in the hall and rats tap-dancing in the bathtub

where we made love on a blanket on the floor
the radio full-blast glutting the room with its jive.

And so I am here and my love is still here
but if I touched you now in your white townhouse
you'd lose your mind   your fingernails would grow ten inches
your hair turn up in peaks and your clothes all shrink
the cat would nosedive out the window
the dishes would crack in the cupboard
the floorboards would warp and turn red
your lawyer would choke on his pipe
and outlaw you right on the spot.

I cannot live in your white townhouse
like some lunatic kept in the attic
a trunk you peek in but will not open
a lover lost on the way
to your white townhouse
where in your room full of cartons
you spin and spin and spin
not sure that you'll ever move in
eyeing me with panic like a getaway horse
equipped for destruction   dreams woven in my mane
to carry you back to the dark country.

The Hippopotamus

*Just as the sun and moon cannot
be reflected in cloudy water, so the
Almighty cannot be reflected in a
soul obsessed with the idea of 'me
and mine'. — Sri Ramakrishna*

Yesterday I saw two slick-backed
bloatsome hippopotami gallop from the mud-
pack of their pen inside the zoo.
Their leggy stumps wiggled feverishly
as their stomachs bumped along the dust.
They have so much to carry with them
everywhere they go   consumer blimpies,
They need a vacation from digestion.

Oh to be an egret   to make a run for it
— I heard one burp   confidentially —
and flap by night to dark Tasmania
where they could never find
or saddle me with fat I'd left behind
fat that clogs the skull and makes me sink:
they'd have to dump it in the river
they would know what to do either
with sacks and sacks of hippopotami me-fat.

I've seen the hypo hippos that gallop
with brains as small and nervous as a shrimp
that lug the tons of world they've eaten.
I've seen them gallop and then wallow
wallow until they were settled well
inside the mud-pools of themselves
with only their shoe-tongue ears peeked
pert above the water   sloshing fears and
listening to the sky they could not swallow.

33

The Ascension of Our Lady of the Missed Bus

Tossing up extravagant handfuls
of promises/a confetti of bus transfers
you never bother to grab hold of one

as they flutter down all around you
a litter of empty paper cups
crumpled around a broken watercooler.
As faces turn slowly away   eyes
glancing down to the ground
in disappointment   you sit cross-
legged   arms folded in your heap
of bits   wondering what happened.

Sometimes when squirrels thrash
through thick piles of leaves
in a panic scratching in search
of buried nuts in forgotten places
I can smile at you in your flurry
of missed appointments/lost keys
unanswered letters/abandoned work
this cluttered racetrack you circle.

And when these leaves are burned
smoke curling under sturdy oaks
I can see the vaporous fingers
of trapped spirits sprung free —
up there with St. Teresa gliding
absentmindedly: fences/branches
telephone poles/the whole world
sliding through their curved hands
as they catch clouds and let the rest go.

34

People Who Hate Their Mothers Love

People who hate their mothers love the sea.
People who think fondly of their mothers
and can be wrapped roundly by the cameo-image
of her face   the flowered apron   the worn
pair of orthopedic oxfords   the tombstone
in the sun where they have left her   for good

often drive by the ocean and can be interested
even vaguely in where they're going or what
they plan to do: they do not stop the car
abruptly   pour out of the door leaving
the lights on   the keys in   the passengers
stunned and waiting aloud in the back seat —
lunge and scramble across the stretch of sand
with untied shoes   flapping their coat-tails
like a wounded sea-gull with broken wings

and stand hypnotically stoned at the cruel
devouring edge of the warm forgiving rhythm
of that hurt remembered smile   always
                                        always

The Shoebox

What was it you kept in that shoebox
the white shoebox on the closet's top shelf?
What is it that has kept you so long
Father? in the box filled with photographs
of the concentration camps you liberated
the box that trembles like Pandora's
with a thousand black moths beating
against a blackened screen: the mute
tremulous scream   16-millimeter
with the sound shut off.

When Patricia and I slipped into your room
to take it from the shelf and deal
the photographs out like playing cards
on the floor

this trench to me
that heap to you

that bit of hair
this bit of bone

when we dealt it out like the fortunes
children squat-legged on the rug
official details of official skeletons

we always came across
the dog-eared one of you
hunched in a belted coat
squinting and standing aside
to help into a transport van
the wizened prisoner nearby

36

who'd just lived four years
like an animal in a box

who beckons you from the shelf
shuffled back into a shoebox
which I have seen you open
and close behind closed lids
the jerky grainy footage
that loops through your mind
the shoebox in the closet
where you keep all your pain.

I remember the smell of must
from the old German armband
I tried to have cleaned
at the cleaners one day;
the feel of kerosene and ash
on that grimy red rag
of a huge Nazi flag
big as a living-room rug;
the dark steel-foundry weight
of that black bludgeon luger
dead as a brick in your drawer
of the souvenir sword hung over my bed
the contained vision of hideousness
hung all over the house.

I have seen you try to rest
like someone who has just cleaned the house;
like someone who has just cleaned the world
who knows there is no rest you sometimes rest
where I have put you   in a white shoebox
in which you sit forever now

staring into a white shoebox in your lap
fascinated to rearrange the cards
in a losing hand of solitaire
played over and over again

that you cannot win   I cannot win
but box within box within box
is put away

          is never put away.

Presenting Eustacia Beauchaud: Ward 3

Eustacia Beauchaud
combed her bozzo
red wig into the Frenchiest
of twists and never missed.
Shot down from Geriatrics
for alleged obscene advances
on a twice-stumped catatonic
she cousined all the kookies
on the spot and said her name
meant good and hot.

In faded brocade she flung
her years all seventy-six
down the echoless hall
of Acutely Disturbed.
With a fox-trot flutter
and a revlon wink
she gave us the word
that you're only as young
as you think   which lit
a few lima-bean eyes
dampened by months of therapy
who caressed the gift
incomprehensively
then let it drop.

With rouge as thick as licorice
and some lipstick oulala
and that slightly ompah strut
(her spirits all played tubas)
she told us she was Lady Levee
and had spooned with Old Man River —

39

a plantation queen she had been
aunt of the mayor of New Orleans:

       If I had my d'rathers
she sang
       I'd rather be down in old Louisiana.

The happy thump of her jazz piano
cured the bristly wino up the corridor
who gurgled her repetoire constantly
somewhere hot deep in his throat.

Evenings mounted like bordello
brawls down in Recreation Therapy.
A southern belle forgets like hell
I heard her hoot at the TV premiere
of *Hush . . . Hush, Sweet Charlotte*
as she was being helped to the toilet.

Always around Individual Lock Up
time she would tell the story ending
pull his tail the nigra told me
that's how you get a horse to work
and then slap herself into a giddy-up with
       We're just twenty-five minutes from Canal Street
       Let's go see the parade.
While orderlies jangled keys she finaled
by raising the beautiful varicose blue

of her leg to the keyboard to pick out Dixie
with her spiked heel of her pointed shoe
and then the black boys in white
would put her to bed
for the night.

Tyger! Tyger!

I hear the buckles rattle from the bed
wheeled in after midnight next to mine
and know the straps
could snap at any time
to hurl the madman
biting on my back.
I hear his nerve-clenched teeth
explode into the mattress
and see between the cowhide and the sheet
muscles strain like wires through paper flesh.
The floor around our beds
is spotted with the spittle of his hate:
the heavy padlock clangs in speech
so primitive that reptiles
crowd into his mouth
which makes no words
nor knows no way
but burning.

Bound by the leather strap cut into his stomach
bound by the hard metallic table by a taste tied hard
in his mouth   he turns toward the wall groaning
within me   his face forming in my thin hands
my boy's beard bristling
with his fever as we seem
drunk into each other
drawn into the father-breath
that breathed us both
tiger and lamb room-
mates in bedlam:
the ward is inside
out.

The room is dark
sleek and tight
and cringes like an animal to strike
he and I the gristled eyes
which cannot see each other
but move in the skull's willful sway
together.

Words Written During a Full Eclipse of the Moon

The moon is a door.
Don't open it.

Starfish dry
on the palm-tree stump:
the sea has withdrawn
like a song that's gone
back in my mind
leaving words stranded.

The moon is a door.
Don't open it.

The blood-red eye
of the big paper fish
in the sky blinks
at me through the trees.

The moon is a door.
Don't open it.

The door is a moon
to keep shut.

New Year / St. Mark's Church

January 1, 1970
New York City

Wearing the wind like a worn shawl
she stumbled into the church we slept in
dwarfed and warted as a night vegetable.
The old woman in the white bakery dress
fretted in and out of the rows of pews
poking a candle long as a broomstick
under every bench and into every corner
sweeping the shadows in the dark of St. Mark's
for a pin or a purse or an irreplaceable button
the raw fingers of her sparrow-boned hands
wringing and twisting to knit out her loss.

As she quarrelled loudly with herself
New Year's morning woke and wept
in the stained-glass face of St. Augustine.
I felt all of the city turn back the covers
from last night's bed of glass and ashes
and move in streets of moaning sleep-walkers
beside this winter spirit on her morning rounds
her knotted face whimpering at each throat
as over and over they said to each other

somehow   friend   we have slipped through
each other's fingers and fallen back again
with empty hands into rooms of crowded absence

where she searches   her breath a beard of ice
stepping over the bundled bodies of children
asleep with their arms around each other
in a chain wrapped around the earth
that will not break   on New Year's morning
for you   for me   will not give way.

The White Tuxedo

I wore a white tuxedo
to my sister's wedding
white tie white tails
white hat white cane:
I gave the bride away.
They drove off in a tan
ford they barely could
afford to kitchenettes
and dripping silverware
and a couple of nice dinners
with the couple down the block.

I wear a white tuxedo
when I visit old girl friends
and always their new oldmen
smile   gesture   ask me in
to watch the lady bake
rap books on group psychology
and stir the soup awhile.
Next week there is a party
why don't I stick around?

Like a phantom escapee
from a Busby Berkeley set
I wear a white tuxedo
and stride low like Groucho
across the sad bridges
where white sea-gulls flash
and chorus as they feed.

No tragic black sombrero
left for me to wear through
ghost towns of pay telephones
down corridors of coke machines.
No more severe French movies
chainsmoking in the back row
no scorpion in my boots
no *bodas de sangre* please.

I wear a white tuxedo
so everyone can see.
I wear a white tuxedo
and smile like Howdy Doody
doing the kickstep of my solitude
tapdancing a slow swan song
in color   real-life   three-d
with a trick-mirror carnation
pinned to my lapel.

I wore a white tuxedo
to my sister's wedding.
I held onto the bride
as I gave myself away.
Then skipped out through
the throng upsetting cakes
and buckets of champagne
to walk my white tuxedo down
the darkest street I know.

Why We Love Bloomingdale's

is the same reason we love
2nd Avenue at 3 A.M.
Because little Lithuanian soup shops
that smell like urinals and
the pervert playpens (old men
dirty in Girls' Underwear
drag queens in Ladies' Accessories
and sodomists in Sporting Goods)
at Bloomingdale's

                and the Pole
who curses as he hands back change
on 2nd Avenue where there is no change

can read us like a book.
Because the cold lapis lazuli
of this drive   this perfection
scaling icy alps of words
to stand looking out at all
like astronauts and alchemists
is some Faustian gyp

and it is love at first sight
to drop from such heights

onto a revolving stool
and swallow horrible hot coffee
as the world swallows you.

To have a cigarette: you have to laugh.

Tarantella

Principessa wears a safety jacket
tucked inside her velvet capelet.
She trusts the captain's aptitude
but waits a great deluge with relish.

She languishes on deck all day
playing José Greco record albums —
in the mute ennui of the sea
she needs to hear the clicking castanets

and see herself in flaming Spanish silk
a hot-tongued devilled dervish of the deep
throwing tantrums with tarantula passion
stomping heels and slashing at the shoreline.

She knows she's never left her destination.
Her future's all behind her: the rest excursion.
She rehearses love behind a bamboo curtain
and sits and sips the icy drinks she's bought.

The Famous Zen Master

I meet the famous Zen Master
in a plain white room
in Brooklyn and
he is smiling.

I drag in my badly band-
aged panama suitcase
dump it at his lily feet
show him my Tarot cards
dirty socks train schedules
smudged notebooks and polar-bear
sweater. I pull out my aspirins
my alarm clock and my shades.

I empty my suitcase
all over the famous Zen Master
and he is smiling.
I want him to tell me where
want him to tap me good
to shake me in the light.

And so I meet
the famous Zen Master
and he is smiling.

He lights a filter cigarette
and says *here schmeer*
and I drop dead
into his smile.

White Peacocks
(to be read in the bookstore)

> *White peacocks and wilted*
> *orchids. . . . But why am I*
> *telling you all this? I*
> *don't even know your name.*
> — *Great Garbo in* Grand Hotel

Supposing you're to take me home:
I must come on like a crash truck
shrill above the sound of traffic
to make you pull over to the side

but what if this tired monkey-haired whore
scraping down Market Street at 6 A.M.
with stockings stuffed in her pocket
were to lean on you the story of her life

would you be ready? Or the elevatorman
at the Bank of America with his cigar
spittle and his toilet-brush mustache
would you pull over for him?

Or my Aunt Olga who dusts bric-a-brac
all day and dreams of being Lucille Ball:
no one has ever pulled over for her.
I pass you every day on your way to work

to the grocery   to the goddam dentist's
my face in a fist or round with a smile
I flag you down with my bright red pajamatop
but never one gesture   one wink   one word.

Now here you are sneaking in this bookstore
in your anonymous jacket this anonymous day
to have a peek at the poetry section
the emotional fuck books   to get a heart-on.

The very same words I would gladly
have pressed under your eyelids   into your palm
had you just looked at me or held out your hand.
But now you have it   the goods   take it

to wherever you go with such things:
I'm still at the typewriter if you need me.

Mardi Gras / Grandmothers
Portrait in Red and Black Crayon

As I see them now and then
one was fat and one was thin
one pushed me out   one held me in.

One created family disgraces
dyed her hair red and danced
her way to Acapulco making
clown lipstick faces.
The other wore mourning
and old creole laces

the two grandmothers I had.

            *   *   *

My Irish grandmother
big Nana of the rose hats
and spaghetti-strap dresses
danced on Mardi Gras floats
until she was seventy-five
with her bonbon hair-do's
and her high-gloss Plymouth
and her hot hotel suite
with her great dripping chins
a languishing sea turtle
in the Parade of Isis.

Ji-my Ji-my
she would siren to me
over the flambeau-carriers
from her tinsel perch

as lush Queen of the Nile.
And I would be hoisted up
smacked with a bourbon kiss
and showered with a gob
of gorgeous glass light.

*　　*　　*

My French grandmother gripped me tight
wrapped her old salvation coat
around her parchment face
and held me back from slipping
into the streams of flambeau-carriers
oh I could march with them all night.
Hip-swaying flame bandits
prancing in a Dixie highstep
rhythm that made my feet
start tapping on the curb.

Mémère wanted it to be Ash Wednesday
to get back to her washing load.
She liked to see the first communions
filing into church in starched white frills.
She liked to think the Virgin Mother
had held pins in her mouth while hemming them.

But I would always buck loose
to follow Nana's gargoyle smile
and jig with packs of black kids
clamoring for kewpies in mid-air

until I shouldered back and sank
into the surf of cat-calls as
flambeaus streaked off around the block
and broken beads crackled everywhere.

*   *   *

And I knew that she'd be standing there
shadowed under street lamps in her coat
waiting in the rubbled paper trash
her collar buttoned high around her throat

knew that she would take my outstretched hand
hot from grabbing glass beads from the floats
take the dazzled face   the jazzed-out legs
take the eyes that panicked through the crowd

and with the votive candle of her heart
lead her flambeau boy the dark way home.

Mr. & Mrs.

1

Oh Mr. Potato-Head Man
your neck folds over
your starched white collar
like hot baked ham.

Your carrot-beak nose is askew
your ears are on backwards
and your green plastic spaghetti
legs just can't keep up with you.

You huff and you bluff
but can't pack away enough
of that good old American stew
and you will never have enough

and there's nothing you can do
your potato-head spiked on
the dollhouse red sedan and
rotting in the carport's morning sun.

2

Your wet set hair bulbed
in a nimbus of steamed air
in your bright white-flowered
pontifical hot hat you stare

back at the big lush beauty magazine
making faces at the made-up face
of the ad's glad pant-suit queen
enticing *you* to flounce and fluff.

Tomorrow you give up mayonnaise.
Perspiration makes your hair dye run
across the face that beauty once began.
You choose becoming shades. You have become.

French-Quarter Bar Fugue
Corner St. Louis and Chartres–then down to Decateur

1
Maspero's Exchange

Great-grandpère
Glaudot
sold cigars
at Maspero's.
At dusk his darkie
cook would go
barefoot down
the Esplanade
to Ramparts past
the slave exchange.

He married Mémère off
to Tennessee society
but kept the younger sister home
for bedpan work and normal school
(she made the children laugh one day
to see a black at school)
and to lug the sideboard crystal set
from eight to four room vacancies.

Note: Maspero's Exchange and the Napoleon House are two historic
buildings in New Orleans located directly across from each other on
the corner of St. Louis and Chartres Streets. Maspero's, originally a
slave exchange, was at one time the tobacco shop and residence of
my great-grandfather. The Napoleon House was intended to be elegant
quarters for the Emperor-in-exile by patriots plotting his escape from
St. Helena. Both buildings, like the Acropolis, a hang-out for Greek
sailors on Decateur Street, are now popular bars.

Dark   dark is the stain
left at Maspero's Exchange.
The walls are white and
pastel champagne bubbles
frizzle from a tipping tumbler
tattooed on the bar-room
window panes

so black the stain.

Inside a silky bouffant Negro
tilts a tray of drinks to tables:
above his smoothly vermouth movements
attic woodwork worms with vermin
generations cotton-fed and fat
nest inside the skull of Maspero
and the enamel pitcher of père Glaudot
these glints of paleness embering
around the sockets swilling darkness

while downstairs there is flickering
some antique dance upon the walls
thick peels of whitewash flaking
with the heat of summer nights.

2

Napoleon House

Wood strum the waiter
from the door to the bar
that aristocratic penguin
in the rumpled white shirt
and looped bow-tie
toothless   listless

with the shoe-shined grace
of the emperor who never
showed up but died
on St. Helena while the creoles schemed.

Napoleon Napoleon
you maudlin melancholian
slumped against the table
in a dignified drunk
spectacles fallen
into your beer
wishing you were anywhere else
but here.

In winter I remember
a corner wrapped in amber
and Brahms that swirled
around the room
like brandy in a goblet
and summer-feathered light that fell
like ferns upon the patio

where glasses empty slowly.

Time rides the heavy mahogany blades
of the lugubrious overhead fan
which drags thoughts in a drugged whir
down toward the chink of ice floating
in the foam of a brandy Alexander.
The waiter eternally polishing glass
and reading a yellowed news-sheet
stands ceramically still near the clock
which always reads midnight or noon

while all around are lingering
in antique portraits on the walls
glares of exiled princes waiting
swift returns to buried thrones.

3

The Acropolis

Opium Rose
swings her milk-thick tits
in Greek juke rhythms.
Both of them are mothers
but she's been fixed.
In stretching pink cashmere
she scoops up bottles
empties ashtrays
and slow-eyes sailors
with a parched ruby smile.

Behind the bar
she smashes glass
and pours out ouzo
then kicks her way
through oyster shells.
She knows the words
but seldom sings them.

While college twiglets
jingle metal bracelets
and tap their feet
to the *zeibékiko*
(the dance meant
only for one man)

and aegean shadows
unfurl against lime neon
to hiss swoop and swallow
in their strange ballet
the checkered belt-loop dates
disappear into the men's room
where around the Greek graffiti
they find a plastic lily
jammed into the vent
of the prophylactics machine.

Afterglow

A speedy taxi atmosphere
in this gaudy gypsy wagon
bouncing down the hill
with stacks of records playing
pots of water boiling
for a tableful of teacups
tilting toward the floor
lipped cigarettes lighting
to the striking of a match
100 watts streaking
through the red silk scarf
draped across the lampshade.

Rings flashing/bracelets rattling
talk tapping out a rhythm
that is hot honey hot.
She is Annie Oakley
she is Theda Bara
she is little girl
who is lost lost lost
a ricochet of motions
with our hair all tossed.

At night
after making love
quiet   barely touching
electric heater humming
on soft white skin
street light patterned
through the panes
across her faceless face:

it is frightening
lying here
sometimes so close
it scares me
lying here.

Rush

kisses like secret pockets in the snow
and then suitcases   the train   aboard   *adieu*
alone after love on a local to the city
alone after first love   alone like before
your face against the cold train pane
your eyes asking questions of windows
of now and forever   of waves and their crests
from the platform I'm waving   fading away
my hands slipping from you past trees *(faster)*
past billboards *(faster)* past bridges
(faster) the train gaining speed *(your life
has begun)* pushes and spews in a chorus
(your life it is over)   a coliseum of cheers
crowds are standing   red banners unfurling
this is your moment   take what you want
forget all the rest   the world is on fire

    VIVA

        VIVA

            VIVA

                VIVA

viva past Hicksville   viva past caring
viva Grand Central   viva the train jolts
viva your feet move   viva the fountain
inside you bursts high as the arc of Times Square

Arguments with the Woodcutter

Living too hard   too fast:
for the first time I notice
the slow tributaries of age
webbing my face as I glance
into the rear-view mirror
of a wood-truck hitch-hiking
north to the mountain resort.

I wait while two stocking-
capped trolls in redwood fairy-
land   woodcutters by trade
argue with the mean old
shrivelled-bean-faced man
who screeches he was cut
short by half a cord. . . .

> Your truck isn't big enough
> to carry all the wood you owe me.
> I've been cheated!
> I've been gypped!
> All these chips
> all this sap-wood
> ain't much but a buncha kindling!

He rasps and fumes as the woodcutters
lumber on back to their truck swinging
heavy glinting blades sharp as scythes.
The chips aren't on their shoulders.
They just chop and stack the stuff
breed hounds   eat oatmeal and marry young.
How can you argue with time's work done?

The city gleams like embers to the south.
Here at the end of Sherman's Trail where
the paths of ash   the rapid-fire explosions
of the years have left me: I will stay.
Here in the land of the sleeping bear
the warm soup bowl and fireside stare
here in this season of the soggy log

I'll rest. At this place called River's
Nest. I see nothing before has caught.
It was all kindling   a bright display
of blazing bark. The core is charred
but cold   growing old   after all untouched
by so very much.
                              That's what burns me up.

12 Positions of Love

one   *the spoons*

You lie like two spoons
fit into each other
like two tucked shells
between which the sea
will not wash
a crescent a curve
something bent close
around itself breathing
like a single animal
breathing.

two   *the snails*

You lie like two crescents
bent away from each other
like a man with the base
of his spine against a mirror
from which he is slowly
curling away from himself
into himself.

three   *the shadow*

You place a cup on the table
and fill it half full of coffee.
She places a cup on the table
and fills it half full of coffee.
You look back over your shoulder
and smile (frown).

four   *the silence*

She lies naked in the middle of the floor
her hands bent over her head.
You stand in your raincoat
in a corner facing the wall.

No one is heard to speak.

five   *here*

You slowly touch the back
of her neck while her hand
slowly brushes your stomach.
There is still
               wine to drink.

six   *there*

You slowly touch the back
of her neck while she
stares out of the window.
Words spilled yesterday lie
like dirty socks around the room.

seven   *other people*

You talk across to her
alone as on the telephone.
There is only the dial tone
of a broken connection.

eight   *the cloud*

     The temptation is to put
     a fist through the pane
     that grows darker between you
     but every breath clouds
     the glass like a mirror.
     In the end you are facing yourself:
     you want to see through
     but you can't
     you just can't.

nine   *the river*

     You are a river
     emptying into her ocean.
     It is never over
     not even after the covers
     are pulled back over:
     she waves through you
     though you do not move.

ten   *waiting*

     You hold hands so tight
     because no one can say
     what has been said.
     The table cloth is crumby
     and no one has an appetite.

eleven   *after*

    Do you know what
    an empty room feels like?
    The light inside the refrigerator
    does go out

    though you could never believe it.

twelve   *again*

    Everything changes.
    You learn it the hard way.
    Three years later
    with nothing to say.